H

OXFORD *playscripts*

Series Editor – Bill Lucas

Adrian Flynn

Hot Cakes

Oxford University Press

Oxford University Press, Walton Street, Oxford OX2 6DP

Oxford   New York
Athens   Auckland   Bangkok   Bombay
Calcutta   Cape Town   Dar es Salaam   Delhi
Florence   Hong Kong   Istanbul   Karachi
Kuala Lumpur   Madras   Madrid   Melbourne
Mexico City   Nairobi   Paris   Singapore
Taipei   Tokyo   Toronto

and associated companies in
Berlin   Ibadan

Oxford is a trade mark of Oxford University Press

Hot Cakes © Adrian Flynn, published by
Oxford University Press, 1991
Reprinted 1994, 1995
Activities © Adrian Flynn 1991
This collection © Oxford University Press, 1991

All rights reserved. This publication may not be reproduced, stored, or transmitted in any forms or by any means, except in accordance with the terms of licences issued by the Copyright Licensing Agency, or except for fair dealing for the purposes of research or private study, or criticism or review, as permitted under the Copyright, Designs and Patents Act, 1988. Enquiries concerning reproduction outside these terms should be addressed to the Permissions Department, Oxford University Press.

A CIP catalogue record for this book is available from the British Library
ISBN 0 19 831273 3

Typeset by Pentacor PLC High Wycombe, Bucks

Printed in Great Britain at the University Press, Cambridge

Contents

Characters	7

The Play: Hot Cakes	
Act 1	9
Act 2	51

Activities	71
Women and Work	72
'You Are What You Read'	76
Divorce	77
Chainstores	79
Takeover	81
All Power Corrupts	82
News Story	83
Child Labour	84
Day-dreams and Ambition	86
Drama Ideas	88
Performing 'Hot Cakes'	90
What the Playwright Says	91
Acknowledgements	93

Characters

Mrs Foster	*A pleasant but rather nervous woman, recently divorced.*
Maria Foster	*Her younger daughter. Early teens. Very hard-headed.*
Elaine Foster	*The elder daughter. Late teens. Hopelessly in love with Rick Beck.*
Lenny	*A trainee baker. Obsessed with science fiction.*
Clare	*Maria's best friend. Very loyal.*
Patty de la Tour	*Another friend. Very extrovert and theatrical.*
Vicky **Tracy**	*Two more friends. Skateboard fanatics.*
Rick Beck	*The ruthless owner of Beck's Bakeries.*
Mr Bunthorne	*The Lord Mayor. Nice but extremely greedy.*
Mrs Bunthorne	*His rather short-sighted wife. A health inspector.*
Mary Bunthorne	*Their short-tempered daughter.*
Archibald Snokes	*Mary's fiancé. Timid.*
Wedding Guests	

No. of speaking roles 13
Male roles 4
Female roles 9

Act 1

Scene 1

A street. **Mum** *and* **Maria** *enter.*

Mum   Thank heavens that's all over.

Maria   How do you feel, Mum?

Mum   I feel fine about the divorce, love. It's . . .

Maria   What?

Mum   Taking over one of the shops that terrifies me.

Maria   It'll be great.

Mum   I know you think so. But what do we know about bakeries? Dad handled all of that.

Maria   We'll learn.

Mum   Will we?

Maria   Of course we will. And remember, we've always got Lenny to help us.

Mum   *(Laughs)* Oh yes.

They exit.

Scene 2

The kitchen of a small bakery shop. There are some cupboards and a couple of ovens. There is also a phone. **Lenny** *is cleaning around the ovens with a scrubbing brush and bucket of water. He opens an oven door and recoils in mock horror.*

Lenny   Aargh! The Swamp Thing from Outer Space!

He takes out a mouldy old loaf and starts fighting it as **Mum** *and* **Maria** *enter. He doesn't see them.*

Die, bread bun!

Maria   Hello Lenny.

Lenny   *(Embarrassed)* Oh, hello Maria, Mrs Foster . . . I was cleaning up.

Mum   It seems so empty without your father. We'll never get it working without him.

Maria   Of course we will, won't we?

Lenny   Oh, aye.

Mum   Are you sure you don't want to go to my husband . . . my ex-husband's new shop?

Lenny   If it's all the same to you, I'd rather stick here.

Mum   You might find yourself out of a job sooner than you think.

Maria   Think positive, Mum.

Lenny   Exactly.

Maria   With me and Lenny doing the baking, the shop'll have a brilliant reputation.

Mum   Do you think so?

Maria	I'm sure so. Cakes, buns, teacakes, scones, we'll make the best in Britain. We'll expand the sandwich delivery service to cover the whole town, the whole of the county . . .
Lenny	The whole of the universe! We'll be delivering tuna salad sandwiches to Venus.
Maria	Lenny!
Lenny	Sorry. I get a bit carried away sometimes.
Mum	It'd be marvellous if it worked.
Maria	Of course it'll work. But first, we've got to think of a new name for the shop. After all, it's a different business now Dad's gone.
Mum	What should we call it?
Maria	Something short and snappy.
Lenny	'Piranha Fish' . . . They're short and snappy.

Maria and Mum give Lenny a withering look.

Maria	I've got it – 'Bites'!
Mum	That makes us sound as though we're vampires.
Lenny	'Intergalactic Sandwiches'!
Mum	That's a bit of a mouthful.
Lenny	So are my sandwiches.
Maria	Everybody think.

They all concentrate hard. We can see the effort on Lenny's face.

Lenny	Crumbs, this is hard.
Maria	That's it!

Mum	Crumbs!
Maria	You're brilliant, Lenny.
Lenny	Am I?
Maria	This shop is hereby officially known as 'Crumbs'.
Lenny	I'll make a sign for it.
Maria	And we'll get things ready to open tomorrow.
Mum	We'll never be ready.
Lenny	It's all clean.
Mum	But there aren't enough of us to get all the bread and cakes ready. If only Elaine would help.
Maria	Some hope. Elaine's too wrapped up in that greasy boyfriend of hers.
Mum	We can't do it all ourselves.
Maria	Mum, I hope you don't mind, but with it being the summer holidays, I've asked one or two friends from school if they could help us out a bit.
Mum	Maria, you know we can't afford to pay anyone . . .
Maria	They'll do it for free. It's better than hanging round the house all day.
Mum	But that's not right. Getting people to work for nothing.
Maria	If the business takes off, we can pay them back.
Mum	I suppose so.
Lenny	Here, you've not asked that tall one to help have you?
Maria	Patty? Yes, why?

ACT ONE

Lenny I'm off to paint the sign. She's batty.

Maria We need all the help we can get.

Lenny exits.

Mum You know, Maria, I'm beginning to think it might just work after all.

Scene 3

*The Lord Mayor's house. All we see is the Lady Mayoress, **Mrs Bunthorne**, on the phone, reading over an announcement.*

Mrs Bunthorne Are you sure you've got it all? 'The Lord Mayor and the Lady Mayoress, Mr and Mrs Bunthorne, wish to announce the wedding of their beloved daughter Mary to Mr Archibald Snokes on Saturday 27th of this month.' . . . Bunthorne . . . B-U-N . . . 'N' for 'nuts' not 'M' for 'mother' . . . Do be careful. And that'll be in this week's edition of 'The Bugle'? . . . Splendid.

She puts the phone down.

Scene 4

*The kitchen of the bakery. **Mum** and **Maria** are on.*

Maria Now you'd better inform the solicitor about the change of name.

Mum You are getting bossy.

Maria I'm only being positive.

Mum Very well . . .

She starts to exit as **Patty** *and* **Clare** *enter.*

Mum	Hello girls, thanks for coming.
Clare	It's a pleasure, Mrs Foster.
Mum	I'll see you later. Try and make sure Maria doesn't get too big for her boots.
Maria	What a nerve!
Mum	Bye!
Patty, Clare, Maria	Bye!
Patty	*(Over the top)* This is wonderful, darlings. This place is going to be fan-tastic!
Maria	I hope so. I was about to start baking bread.
Patty	Bread! Fan-tastic! I see french sticks, I see sesame seed buns, I see fluffy little rolls . . .
Clare	Patty.
Patty	Yes, Clare?
Clare	Put a sock in it.
Patty	Put a sock in it? That's no way to talk to a genius.
Maria	I'm afraid all the work's got to be done by hand. Dad's got all the equipment in his new shop.
Clare	We'll manage.

Maria *takes out a large mixing bowl.*

Maria	Now, how do we make bread?

ACT ONE

Clare   You're the baker's daughter.

Maria   Dad never let us in the kitchen. He said women got in the way.

Clare   The cheek of the man!

Maria   You ought to know how to bake bread, Patty. You do domestic science.

Patty   Yes dear, but I only go there to catch up on my sleep.

Clare   We'll have to experiment, then.

Maria   Right. Well, let's start with the flour.

Patty   *(Taking bag from cupboard)* Is this flour?

Clare   Yes.

Patty   I thought it looked familiar.

Maria   Bung it in.

> **Patty** *starts pouring the flour into the bowl in a very artistic, delicate way.*

Clare   *(Impatient)* Give it here.

> **Clare** *takes the bag and shakes it violently into the bowl, making a great cloud of flour. They all cough.* **Elaine** *enters, dressed to kill.*

Elaine	Having fun?
Maria	We're trying to get the business going again, Elaine. You could lend a hand.
Elaine	I'd love to, but I'm busy.
Maria	Off seeing lover-boy?
Elaine	Never you mind. See you later.

She exits.

Patty	Now, do we put this in the oven?
Clare	You need more than flour to make bread, you know.
Patty	No one told me, dear.
Clare	You've got to put in . . . er . . .
Maria	Yeast! There should be some yeast somewhere.
Patty	What does yeast look like? Animal, vegetable or mineral?
Clare	*(Taking large tin from cupboard)* Is this it?
Patty	Well done.
Maria	How much do we put in?
Patty	Well, there were five kilograms of flour in the bag, so I suppose we ought to put in five kilograms of yeast.
Clare	We haven't got that much.
Maria	Let's see if we can get away with just putting in this one tin.
Clare	Okay. Here's hoping.

She empties the tin of yeast into the flour. All three of them look suspiciously at the bowl.

ACT ONE 17

Maria It looks a bit . . .

Clare Dry.

Patty I know, there's something else we need. I accidentally woke up during Miss Porter's lesson once.

Maria What is it?

Patty Water.

Clare Right.

She exits to fetch a jug of water.

Patty Now isn't that clever of me to remember. I could be a brilliant chef if I wasn't already so talented in every other way.

***Clare** returns with two jugs of water.*

Maria Slosh it in.

***Clare** starts pouring.*

Clare How much?

Patty Ooh, now, let's see. Can I remember?

She tries desperately to think back.

Maria Half a pint, a pint, two pints?

***Clare** starts pouring in the second jug.*

Patty It's coming to me . . . It's on the tip of my tongue.

The bowl is overflowing.

Clare I don't think any more'll fit in.

Patty I've got it! . . . Not too much water, that's what Miss Porter said.

They all look at the mess in the bowl as **Lenny** *enters carrying a sign that reads 'Crumms'.*

Lenny   *(Holding up sign)* There, what do you think?

Maria   You've spelt it wrong, Lenny.

Lenny   You know, I thought there was something funny about it. I couldn't make up my mind whether 'crumbs' had one 'm', or two.

Patty   You've missed out the 'b', darling.

Lenny   The 'b'?

Patty   The 'b'.

Lenny   There's no 'b' in 'crumbs'. It's not 'crum-bes'.
(To Maria) I told you she was batty.

Patty   You know, Lenny, when God was making you, I think he used so much material for the mouth, there wasn't any left over to make you a brain.

Lenny   *(Looking at the bowl)* What on earth's that?

Maria   It's the bread mix.

Lenny   It looks more like the Slime Creature. You should've asked me how to make bread. I'm the one who's worked here before.

ACT ONE 19

Patty   I hope he's better at baking than sign-writing.

Lenny   Come on, I'll show you.

Maria   Okay.

Patty   I think I'd be more use making a proper sign.

She picks up sign and exits.

Lenny   You want to watch her, she'll be putting 'b's all over it. Now, have we got some flour?

Clare and Maria exchange glances, then decide to go along with him.

· ·

Scene 5

A table in a café. Elaine and her boyfriend Rick are seated at a small table, drinking coffee. There is a plate of cakes on the table.

Rick   So, how's your mother?

Elaine   Not too bad.

Rick   Upset by the divorce?

Elaine   It's what she and Dad wanted.

Rick   I suppose she'll be ready to sell the shop soon.

Elaine   I don't know. I don't think so.

Rick   No?

Elaine   I think she's going to have a go at running the business herself.

Rick   What on earth does she know about it?

Elaine	Nothing. It's my little sister who's talked her into it. I think she should sell up. I told her you were interested.
Rick	Only as a favour to you, Elaine. You understand that?
Elaine	Oh yeah. I think it's really lucky you started going out with me just as we were deciding what to do with the shop.
Rick	You know my company is too big to worry about little shops like your mother's normally?
Elaine	Oh yeah. Everyone knows Beck's Bakeries are the biggest in this part of the world.

She takes a cake.

Rick	Not just the biggest, Elaine. We're also the best. And soon we'll be the only bakery, when all the competition has crumbled.
Elaine	*(Spitting out piece of cake)* These cakes are disgusting. This café ought to know better . . .
Rick	*(Picking up a cake)* They're Beck's cakes, Elaine. Delicious. They must be too sophisticated for you.

He stuffs the whole cake in his mouth.

· ·

Scene 6

The kitchen of the bakery. **Clare** *and* **Lenny** *are putting bread tins in the oven.* **Maria** *is on the phone.*

Maria	That's the whole menu . . . Say the 'Dial-a-sandwich' service offers free delivery anywhere in town. If the advert can go in the paper this week . . .
Patty	*(Enters with sign)* Ta-ran-da-ra! Look at this, my darlings!

The sign reads 'Crumbs. Fan-tastic food, fan-tastic prices!' It is very colourful and ornate.

ACT ONE 21

Maria	Sssh! *(On phone)* And you know where to send the bill? . . . That's it. Bye. *(She puts the phone down)* Couldn't you see I was on the phone, Patty?
Patty	Don't get angry with a genius, dear. What do you think of my masterpiece?
Clare	It's . . . eye-catching.
Maria	Not easy to ignore.

Mum enters.

Patty	What do you think of my brilliant sign, Mrs Foster?
Mum	Well . . . it's . . . er . . .
Patty	Yes?
Mum	Unbelievable.
Lenny	Isn't it just? She's been at school all these years and she still doesn't know how to spell 'Crumbs'.
Clare	Don't mind him, Mrs Foster.
Maria	Did you get things sorted out at the solicitors?

Mum	Yes. The shop's registered in its new name.
Maria	I've put an advert in the paper.
Clare	We've got the first batch of bread in the oven.
Lenny	And some baps.
Patty	And I've produced the most wonderful sign in the world.
Mum	Oh dear.
Maria	What's wrong, Mum?
Mum	I'm always suspicious when everything's going well. It usually means something nasty is about to happen.

Rick enters, followed by Elaine.

Elaine	I've brought Rick back, Mum. He said he wanted to meet the family.
Rick	Hello, Mrs Foster.
Mum	Pleased to meet you, Rick. I understand you own Beck's Bakeries?
Rick	*(Looking round)* It's a nice little place you've got here.
Maria	It's not so little.
Rick	How much are you thinking of selling it for?
Mum	Selling it?
Maria	We're not thinking of selling it!
Rick	Come now, Mrs Foster, let's be realistic. You're not really going to try and run the shop, are you?
Mum	I don't know . . .

ACT ONE 23

Rick   There are so many things to worry about. Your overheads, the fuel costs, your basic supplies, transport for the sandwich deliveries, promotion, cash-flow. It's an awful lot to tackle.

Mum   *(Worried)* Well, when you put it like that . . .

Rick   Let's face it: women shouldn't have to worry their pretty little heads about business, should they?

Elaine   Rick's only thinking of your best interests, Mum.

Rick   We'd give a very reasonable price. Very reasonable.

Mum   I don't know . . .

Maria   Wait a minute! Who says women aren't cut out to do business? We are, aren't we?

Patty and Clare   Yes!

Maria   We're going to make a real go of this. You're just afraid of losing customers to us.

Rick   Losing customers to you?

Clare   Everyone knows Beck's cakes are disgusting.

Elaine   They're too sophisticated for you, that's what it is.

Maria   So we don't need your offer, thank you very much.

Rick   *(Coldly)* What a spirited child.

Elaine   Mum, don't listen to her. Rick knows best.

Mum   *(After some thought)* I don't think we will sell, Rick. Not yet, anyway.

Maria   That's right, Mum!

Patty   Hear! Hear!

Rick	Well . . . the best of luck to you . . . *(He goes over to Patty's sign)* Though I must say you've made a bit of an amateurish start. *(To Elaine)* Bye Lambikins.
Elaine	Bye Sugar-plum.

Rick exits.

Patty	*(Almost speechless with rage)* Amateurish! . . . My sign, amateurish!
Maria	I don't know what you see in him, Elaine.
Elaine	You can't be expected to recognize style and class at your age. I think you've all been very silly, turning down Rick's offer. He only made it as a special favour to me.

Elaine exits angrily.

Mum	Oh dear, I hope we haven't upset her too much.
Lenny	I don't trust that Rick one bit. He looks like the evil Lump in 'Revenge of the Martian Potato Peelers'.
Patty	That man is the most opinionated, pompous, idiotic, snivelling, drivelling, over-inflated windbag of an ignoramus that I have ever met!
Lenny	I don't care what you say. I still don't like him.
Clare	He could cause us trouble.
Mum	Do you think so?
Maria	He hasn't the brains to do it. Don't start worrying, Mum.
Patty	*(In a world of her own)* You might as well call Michelangelo 'amateurish'.
Mum	What's that smell?
Lenny	The bread!

ACT ONE

*He and **Clare** dive to take it out of the oven.*

Patty   Or Leonardo da Vinci 'amateurish'.

Mum   Ooh, it smells gorgeous.

***Clare** and **Lenny** put the bread on a worktop.*

Maria   Perfect.

Clare   The proof is in the eating.

Lenny   Everyone try a piece.

He breaks off little pieces of bread to give to everyone.

Maria   It's delicious.

Clare   Fabulous.

Mum   This is as good as Dad baked.

Maria   What do you think, Patty?

Patty   I think . . . he must have been dropped on his head as a baby.

Mum   Rick did have a point, though . . .

Maria   Mum!

Mum   No, really. How can we keep up the sandwich delivery service if we don't have a van any more?

Lenny   Good point.

Maria   I've thought of that.

Mum   Well?

Maria   You'll have to wait until tomorrow to see.

Clare	It's a surprise.
Mum	*(Annoyed)* Who's running this business, Maria, you or me?
Maria	We all are. Please, Mum – wait till tomorrow.
Patty	Don't worry, Mrs Foster, with a genius like me around, you can't go far wrong.
Mum	Very well, but I'm not sure what I'm letting myself in for.
Maria	The time of your life, that's what.

• •

Scene 7

The Lord Mayor's house. **Mr** *and* **Mrs Bunthorne** *are seated. Their daughter* **Mary** *is standing over them, rather menacingly.*

Mary	You've got the bridesmaids organized?
Mrs Bunthorne	Yes, dear.
Mary	And the page boys?
Mr Bunthorne	Yes, dear.
Mary	And the flowers?
Mrs Bunthorne	Yes, dear.
Mary	Announcement in the paper?
Mrs Bunthorne	Went in this morning.
Mary	What about the catering?
Mr Bunthorne	Ah . . .
Mrs Bunthorne	Well . . .

ACT ONE

Mary — Don't tell me you haven't sorted out the catering?

Mrs Bunthorne — It hasn't been easy, dear . . .

Mr Bunthorne — Only the best will do for you.

Mary — Things have come to a pretty pass when the Lord Mayor and his wife can't sort out the catering for their daughter's wedding.

Mrs Bunthorne — We are trying.

Mary — And you being a health inspector, Mother, you must know who the best caterers are.

Mrs Bunthorne — That's the trouble, dear. Most of the bakeries are owned by Beck's now, and you know they're hopeless.

Mary — I can feel one of my tempers coming on.

Mr Bunthorne — Oh no.

Mrs Bunthorne — Please calm down, dear . . .

Mr Bunthorne — We haven't replaced the crockery from the last time.

Mary — Then I want the catering sorted out in the next couple of weeks. Understood?

Mr Bunthorne — Oh yes.

Mrs Bunthorne — Certainly, dear.

Mary — Fine. Now I'm off to tell Archibald what to wear for the wedding. I'll see you later.

She exits.

Mrs Bunthorne — We'll go round town next week. There must be someone who can do the catering for us.

Mr Bunthorne — If we don't find someone, she'll call the whole wedding off and you know what that means.

Mrs Bunthorne	She'll go on living with us.
	Mr and Mrs Bunthorne exchange horrified glances.

Scene 8

The kitchen of the bakery. The next morning. Maria, in white overall and cap, is putting some cake mix into a tray of cake shapes. Clare enters, takes her overall and cap from a peg and puts it on during the following:

Maria	Morning.
Clare	Morning. I thought I was early. What time did you start?
Maria	I don't know . . . I was in here at about half six.
Clare	What?
Maria	I couldn't sleep. I wanted to get started.
Clare	You really want this to work, don't you?
Maria	Yeah, I suppose so . . . I want to prove to Mum that we can cope without Dad.
Clare	Do you miss him?
Maria	I still see him every other weekend.
Clare	Do you miss him living here?
Maria	Sort of.
Clare	Is it better or worse without him?
Maria	I'm glad they're not arguing all the time. But I wish there was some way they could have stayed together.

ACT ONE

Clare I've always wondered what it was like to have a dad. Mine took off before I was two.

Maria It was great.

> *Clare joins in putting out the cake mix.*

Clare Really?

Maria Used to be. In the old days. When Dad came in for tea. He always smelt of bread. It was a nice, clean smell. He'd kiss all of us before we started eating. He was always smiling, especially at Mum. She'd smile back at him when she thought me and 'Laine weren't looking – a secret little smile . . . *(She stops talking)*

Clare What happened?

Maria Somehow they just stopped smiling . . . And one day Dad told us he was leaving. He said he'd make sure we were okay for money. That's when he started the other shop and this one was wound down.

> *Lenny walks on, carrying the 'Crumbs' sign, a step-ladder and hammer and nails.*

Lenny Morning, Earthlings.

> *He takes a fingerful of the cake mix. Maria slaps his hand.*

Maria Get off!

Lenny *(Tasting it)* Not bad. Not bad at all.

Maria It's time you got that sign up outside, so people know we're back in business.

Lenny Hark at Miss Bossy-boots.

Maria Get a move on.

Lenny	*(Like a robot)* Order received. I will proceed to obey.

He exits.

Clare	What do you think'll happen to all this when we have to go back to school?
Maria	I hope Mum'll have got things into the swing of it by then, and will decide to keep it open. She can take someone on to help. The main thing is convincing her it can work.
Clare	*(Lifting cake trays)* These are about ready.
Maria	She needs something to occupy her.

Clare starts putting the cakes in the oven as Patty enters.

Patty	I'm here, darlings.
Maria	You're late.
Patty	Genius is not governed by clocks.
Maria	But a bakery is.
Patty	I had to get my make-up perfect. It takes time.
Clare	But you're only working in here. Mrs Foster's doing the shop.
Patty	I know. But I'm going to be answering the phone, aren't I?
Clare	Yes.
Patty	Well, then. You can hardly expect me to talk to people if I'm not looking at my very best. Now, where's my costume?
Maria	Your overall and cap are on the peg.

Patty looks at them.

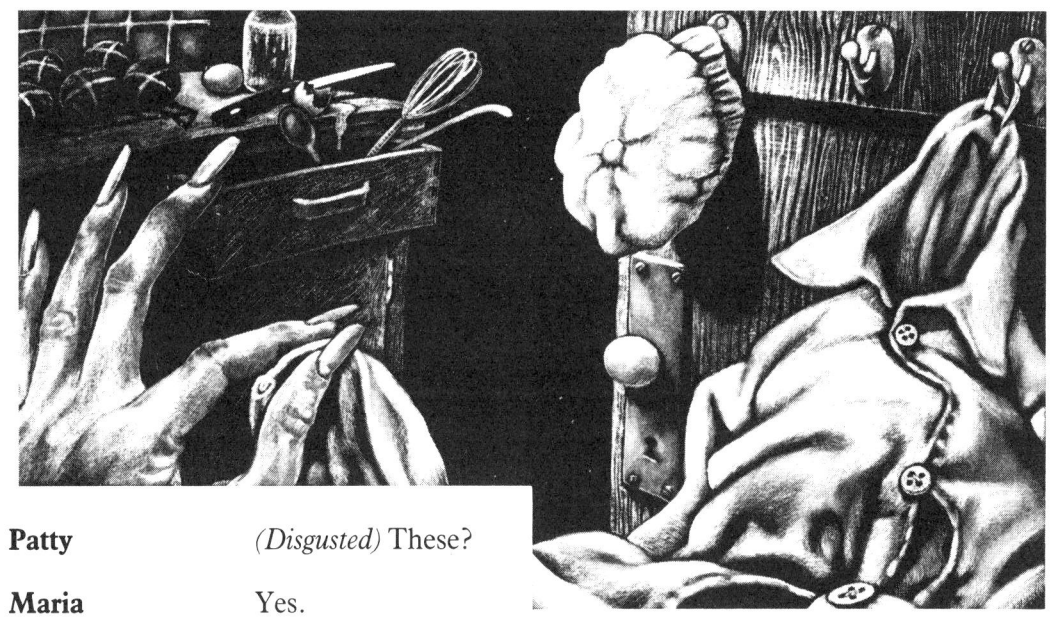

Patty (*Disgusted*) These?

Maria Yes.

Patty But I don't look good in white. It's not my colour at all.

Maria Put them on. Health regulations.

Patty If you insist.

> *Rather grumpily* **Patty** *starts putting on the overalls as* **Mum** *enters.*

Mum Everything all right back here?

Clare Great, Mrs Foster.

Maria How's the shop looking?

Mum Very nice, now we've got everything on display.

Maria Not long to opening.

Mum Maria, what about this delivery service you're supposed to have organized?

Maria	They'll be here any minute.

Lenny enters, carrying step-ladder.

Lenny	I've just been knocked off the ladder by two hooligans on skateboards.
Maria	They've arrived!

Tracy and Vicky enter, skateboards under their arms. They are dressed in leathers or denim.

Tracy	Wotcha!
Vicky	Hiya!
Mum	This is the delivery service?
Tracy	That's right Mrs F. Fastest thing on four wheels.
Vicky	Is something wrong?
Mum	No . . . it's very kind of you to help out . . . only . . .
Tracy	Yeah?
Mum	I'm not sure it's quite the right image for a bakery.
Vicky	What's wrong with our image?
Mum	You do look a bit like Hell's Angels.
Tracy	Exactly.

Vicky and Tracy turn round to show 'Hell's Angel Cakes' printed on the back of their jackets or T-shirts.

Vicky	Hell's Angel Cakes.
Tracy	Help advertise the goods.

Lenny	Hooligans, I call 'em.

*He exits with the ladders, as **Tracy** and **Vicky** give him a nasty look.*

Mum	I'll let you all get on with it then. Good luck.

She exits.

Tracy	So where do we take the sandwiches?
Maria	We're waiting for our first order.

The phone rings. Everyone makes a grab for it, but it rings off before anyone can pick it up.

Patty	May I remind everybody, *I* have been cast in the role of telephonist.

*The phone rings again. **Patty** picks it up very grandly, as **Lenny** re-enters.*

Patty	(*Into phone*) Hello, you are addressing Patty de la Tour . . . Yes, I am speaking from 'Crumbs' bakery, but don't go running away with the idea that I'm a baker. Far from it, darling, I was born to be a star of stage and screen . . . What? . . . Some other time? . . . I see. You'd like to order a sandwich. Very well . . . An egg and cress roll with mayonnaise. White bread? . . . And a Danish pastry to follow? (*Tuts*) Have you thought about all the calories in that little lot? . . . Well, you say you're hungry now, but you'll regret it later, won't you? You'll be putting on inches in all the wrong places and white bread won't do you the least bit of good, will it? . . . No . . . What do I suggest? . . . A couple of crispbread and a slice of cucumber should be adequate . . . Better still, do without anything. That's what I'd do, if I didn't already have the perfect figure . . . All right then? Byeee!

She puts the phone down. Everyone is staring in disbelief at her.

Clare and Maria	Patty!
Patty	Did I do something wrong?

Maria   I'll take the next call.

Patty   I thought I handled it very professionally.

The phone rings.

Maria   Ready everyone? *(She picks up the phone)* 'Crumbs' dial-a-sandwich service, what would you like to order?

*As **Maria** calls out the following orders very fast, **Patty** writes the order down, then passes it to **Clare**, who cuts open a roll, then passes it to **Vicky**, who puts margarine on it before passing it to **Tracy**, who stuffs in the filling. Finally **Tracy** gives the roll to **Lenny**, who puts it in a box.*

... Ham on wholemeal, easy on the mustard ... Tuna salad on rye, plenty of butter ... soft cream cheese and chives in a sesame seed bun ... double egg and tomato ... chicken with salad cream in a bap; chopped liver and onion ... *(She puts her hand over the mouthpiece)* Chopped liver and onion?

Everyone *(As though being sick)* Eurrgh!

Maria   *(Back on the phone)* Two packets of crisps and eight apple strudels to follow. Where to? ... Jacksons' Motors on the High Street ... They'll be there in five minutes. *(She puts down phone)*

Patty   It'll play murder with their figures.

Maria   Have you made up the bill?

Patty   Here.

*Maria takes it and gives it to **Tracy**.*

Maria   Right, ready?

*Lenny holds up two boxes of sandwiches. **Tracy** and **Vicky** stand on their skateboards, 'revving up'.*

Maria Go!

Tracy shoots past Lenny, snatching one box and going straight offstage.

Maria Go!

Vicky does the same with the other box.

Clare Whoo! We're in business!

Lenny and Patty Yeah!

Maria Come on everybody. Back to work.

They all look at her. She's serious.

Come on, get moving.

They all start clearing up as the scene ends.

Scene 9

*The café. **Rick** and **Elaine** are seated at a table, with coffee and cakes. **Elaine** is bravely trying to eat a Beck's cake.*

Elaine *(Struggling)* You know, I think I'm beginning to like your cakes, Rick.

Rick How are things going at your mother's shop?

Elaine Not too badly.

Rick I don't understand it. I didn't think it'd last a week.

Elaine It's my little sister, really. She's quite a businesswoman.

Rick She's a damned nuisance!

Elaine Why? If she can make a success of it . . .

Rick How can she? She won't be able to compete against Beck's Bakeries.

Elaine You sound as though you want her to fail.

Rick Not at all, sweetie-pie. I only want what's best for you and your family. It's just not natural for women to want to go out to work. They're happiest staying at home, looking after the family, while some man takes care of them. You name me one woman who's had a really successful career.

Elaine Ooh, Florence Nightingale, Mother Teresa, Margaret Thatcher . . .

Rick *(Not listening)* You see, you can't. I've only got your best interests at heart, my little candy drop. You do believe me, don't you?

Elaine Oh, yeah.

Rick Have another cake.

Elaine Er . . . no thanks. Too much of a good thing all at once.

Rick *(Getting up)* Then let's get going.

Elaine	Where to?
Rick	To 'Crumbs'. It's about time I had another talk with your mother and little sister.

*He exits, followed by **Elaine**.*

· ·

Scene 10 *Kitchen of the bakery. **Vicky** and **Tracy** are whizzing on and off with sandwiches. **Patty**, **Maria**, **Lenny** and **Clare** are all busy making sandwiches, preparing things for the ovens, etc. **Lenny** holds up a large, misshapen biscuit.*

Lenny	What do you think, everybody?
Clare	What is it?
Lenny	It's obvious.
Clare	Not to me.
Lenny	Listen, you've got gingerbread men and gingerbread women, haven't you?
Maria	Yeah.
Lenny	Well, now you've got gingerbread space fiends with hideous fangs.
Patty	He means he's messed up the gingerbread men.
Lenny	I haven't! It's a new line.
Vicky	I think it's a good idea.
Lenny	You should do. I modelled it on you.
Vicky	Watch it, sunshine.

Mum enters.

Mum We've got a visitor.

Rick enters, followed by Elaine.

Rick My, my, we are busy, aren't we?

Tracy 'Scuse me.

She whizzes past Rick with a box of sandwiches, almost knocking him over, then exits.

Maria Do you want to place an order?

Rick Hardly.

Elaine Rick's come to make a final offer for the shop.

Mum It's a very good offer.

Maria But we're not selling, are we, Mum?

Clare Please don't, Mrs Foster.

Patty Not to that dreadful philistine.

Rick I can understand, you've all enjoyed your little hobby, playing at bakers . . .

Maria We haven't been playing!

Rick So when I turn this place into a real sandwich bar, 'Quick Rick's', I'll take you all on as Saturday girls.

Vicky 'Scuse me.

She shoots past him, almost knocking him over as she exits with a box of sandwiches.

Elaine You can't say fairer than that, can you? Rick's being very generous.

ACT ONE

Rick   I'll find work for all of you. Even this one *(he indicates Patty)* must have some talent. She could do the publicity for 'Quick Rick's'.

Patty   I'd love to.

Maria, Clare and Lenny   What?

Patty   I can see it now, darlings. Big, bright, pink neon lights outside the shop . . .

Rick   Very good.

Patty   Spelling out, 'Quick Rick's . . . makes you sick'.

Mum   Patty!

Maria   I wouldn't work for you if it was the last job on Earth. Beck's Bakeries churn out tasteless, machine-made rubbish.

Clare   We make real bread and sandwiches.

Lenny   Individually crafted Gingerbread Space Fiends.

Mum   I don't know, Maria. Things are going very well now, but when the holidays are over and you've all gone back to school, what's going to happen?

Maria   Mum, can we have a word in private?

Rick   I can't wait all day, you know.

Maria   We won't be long.

                *She goes to one side of the kitchen with **Mum**.*

Mum   He really is offering a reasonable price.

Maria   Mum, if you sell this shop, it won't only be our jobs that disappear, it'll be your independence as well.

Mum   My independence?

Maria	When Dad left, you didn't think you'd ever be able to manage without him, did you?
Mum	I was terrified.
Maria	Well, you've learned how to cope now. We all have. In fact, we're doing more than coping, we're making a real go of this shop. I've never been so proud of you or so glad I've got such good friends. If we let Rick buy this up, we might make some money, but we'll lose all our self-respect.
Rick	*(Loudly)* This is typical, Elaine. Women just can't come to quick, business-like decisions.
Mum	Oh, but we have. We've decided to turn down your offer once and for all, Mr Beck.
Clare	Well done!
Rick	Dear, oh dear. I was hoping I could avoid any unpleasantness, but now I see I don't have any choice.
Maria	Are you threatening us?
Rick	Threatening? Not at all. But I couldn't help noticing the work force here is a little . . . young. I don't think the Health and Safety Inspectors will like that.
Maria	You wouldn't tell them!
Rick	I feel it's my duty. I don't like to see young people exploited this way. I'd've thought you would have known better, Mrs Foster.
Mum	Can't you stop him, Elaine?
Rick	*(To Elaine)* You do understand I'm only acting in the best interests of your little sister and the other children?
Elaine	*(Miserably)* I suppose so.
Rick	I'll arrange for an inspector to call this afternoon. I'll ring again this evening when it's been closed down. Of course, after all this delay,

ACT ONE 41

>the price will have dropped rather a lot. *(To Elaine)* Bye Cutie-lamb!

> *He starts to exit as **Vicky** and **Tracy** re-enter on skateboards, knocking him down. He gets up angrily and walks off.*

Maria   Elaine, how can you go out with him?

Elaine   I'm sorry, I can't help myself.

> *She exits.*

Mum   I'll have to sell the shop now.

Clare   When it was going so well.

Lenny   What'll happen to my space fiends?

Tracy   Why's everyone looking so miserable?

Vicky   Is something wrong?

Mum   The shop's going to be closed down.

Maria   We're all too young.

Patty   Aren't you all forgetting something rather important?

Clare   What?

Patty   You have a genius in your midst.

Lenny   Where?

Patty   Your favourite Aunty Patty and her acting box.

Lenny   I warned you she was batty.

Patty   We're expecting the shop to be closed down this afternoon, because we're all too young, right?

Everyone	Right.
Patty	But suppose by the time the inspector gets here we don't look too young?
Mum	Patty, you're not going to do anything foolish, are you?
Patty	Trust me, I'm a genius. Tracy and Vicky, can you come with me? We've got a special collection and delivery to make.
Tracy	I'm with you.
Vicky	And me.
Patty	*(To the others)* See you soon, darlings.

> ***Patty**, **Tracy** and **Vicky** exit. The rest look at each other in bewilderment.*

Lenny	Batty, absolutely batty.

Scene 11

*The Lord Mayor's house. **Mr Bunthorne** is seated looking through a Yellow Pages Directory. **Mrs Bunthorne** enters, rather short-sightedly.*

Mrs Bunthorne	Have you seen my spectacles, Horatio?
Mr Bunthorne	No, dear. Where did you put them last?

HOT CAKES

Mrs Bunthorne If I knew that, I wouldn't still be looking for them.

Mr Bunthorne No, dear.

Mrs Bunthorne It's really too bad.

Mr Bunthorne What is, dear?

Mrs Bunthorne They want me to go in, though they know it's my day off, and now I shall have to go without my glasses.

Mr Bunthorne You can't go anywhere. You're helping me find a caterer for the wedding.

Mrs Bunthorne You'll have to do it alone, I'm afraid. The chief's very upset. An anonymous phone-call has come in about some poor schoolchildren being forced to work at a shop in Park Street. I've got to go and sort it out.

Mr Bunthorne How am I going to find someone to do the food for Mary's wedding?

Mrs Bunthorne Go to all the bakeries in town and try some of the food at each one.

Mr Bunthorne *(Likes the idea)* Really? Well, I suppose I could try.

Mrs Bunthorne Don't bother going to any of Beck's shops. Their food tastes awful.

Mr Bunthorne Very well dear, don't worry. Of course I shan't enjoy spending all afternoon eating cakes, but you have to make sacrifices for your daughter's wedding, don't you?

Mrs Bunthorne Don't overdo it, Horatio.

Mr Bunthorne No, dear. Goodbye.

She exits. **Mr Bunthorne** *looks back at the Yellow Pages.*

Now where shall I start? I almost wish I hadn't had that fourth helping of sponge pudding for lunch. I've got a lot of hard work ahead of me.

Scene 12

The kitchen of the bakery. **Maria, Clare, Patty** *and* **Lenny** *have been very crudely transformed into old people by putting on white wigs and glasses, and by carrying walking sticks.*
*****Lenny** *is seated on a chair, while* **Patty** *sticks a false moustache on him.*

Lenny Get off! I don't want a false moustache.

Patty You're having one, darling.

Lenny But I'm the only one of us who *is* old enough to be working.

Patty Then you shouldn't look so baby-faced.

Lenny It's tickling.

Maria *(To Lenny)* When the inspector comes, stay on the chair and pretend to be asleep. That'll be the safest thing.

Clare How do I look?

Patty Ancient.

Clare Great.

*****Mum** *enters hurriedly.*

Mum The inspector's here . . . Oh, this'll never work.

Patty Trust me, Mrs Foster, trust me.

Mrs Bunthorne *(Offstage)* May I come in?

Patty *(Ancient voice)* Enter.

As **Mrs Bunthorne** *comes onstage,* **Clare, Maria** *and* **Patty** *become incredibly old and doddery in the way they move and talk.* **Mum** *exits, looking worried.*

ACT ONE

Mrs Bunthorne *(Taken aback, tries to look closely at them)* Good afternoon.

Patty, Clare and Maria Good afternoon.

Mrs Bunthorne I've come to inspect the bakery.

Clare What's she say?

Mrs Bunthorne I'd heard reports there were under-age workers here.

Maria Under-age workers? That'll be young Mildred you're thinking about. *(Points to Clare)* Not a day over seventy-three is young Mildred. Are you, love?

Clare You what?

Maria You're not a day over seventy-three, are you?

Clare Yes, I'd like a nice cup of tea, thank you.

Patty *(To Mrs Bunthorne)* You make yourself at home, deary. We'll get on with making some cakes, if you don't mind. There's a bit of a rush on.

Mrs Bunthorne stands out of the way as, in slow motion, Maria starts stirring a bowl of cake mix. Patty, with a great effort, picks up an individual greaseproof cake shape.
Maria tries to spoon some cake mix into it, but they are both so doddery, they keep missing. Finally, Patty sets off to the ovens with the small cake. It's a great effort to walk so far and the cake gets heavier and heavier.

Clare Keep going, dear.

Maria You can do it.

Clare Not much further.

>*Patty struggles to the oven, which **Clare** opens with a great effort. **Patty** puts the cake in, **Clare** closes the oven door, and all three girls collapse on the worktops, exhausted.*

Maria Time for a rest.

Mrs Bunthorne *(Going over to Lenny)* What does this gentleman do?

Patty Old Mr Tompkins? *(To Maria)* What does Mr Tompkins do?

Maria Not very much. He's been like that for two weeks now.

Clare We rather think he's dead.

Patty But he hasn't started to smell yet.

Mrs Bunthorne Is there anyone else working here who might be under age?

Patty Only the delivery girls.

Maria Myrtle and Mavis.

Patty They're a couple of young tearaways, aren't they, Mildred?

Clare *(Looks at watch)* Half past three.

Maria Here they are.

>***Vicky** and **Tracy**, also in wigs, enter, propelling themselves on their skateboards with walking frames.*

Patty Afternoon, girls.

Tracy and Vicky Afternoon.

Maria *(Handing them a box of sandwiches each)* Can you take this order to thirty-two, Mafeking Gardens?

Tracy When do they want it by?

ACT ONE

Maria A week next Thursday.

Vicky Should just make it, then.

> *Tracy and Vicky skate off.*
> *Lenny, tickled by the moustache, starts making noises as though he is about to sneeze.*

Mrs Bunthorne I can't really see what the complaint was about. None of you is exactly a spring chicken.

> *Patty has gone across and put her finger under Lenny's nose to stop him sneezing.*

Maria So you won't be closing down the bakery?

Mrs Bunthorne No. In fact, your food smells so good, I was going to ask if you'd be interested in doing the catering for my daughter's wedding. My husband's the Lord Mayor. It'd be very good publicity for you.

Maria What do you think, girls?

Patty *(Taking finger away from Lenny's nose)* I think it's a spiffing idea.

Maria What about you, Mildred?

Clare I've told you once. Half past three.

Lenny *(About to sneeze)* Ah . . . ahh . . .

> *Patty quickly puts her finger under his nose.*

Maria *(To Mrs Bunthorne)* That's fine, then. If you leave the details with my mother . . . er . . . my other assistant in the shop, we'll do it with pleasure.

Mrs Bunthorne Agreed.

> *She shakes hands with Maria, then with Clare and then with Patty. As Patty takes her finger away from Lenny's nose, Lenny gives*

an almighty sneeze, covering his nose with his hands.
As he takes his hands away, the moustache comes with them. **Mrs Bunthorne** *stares at him.*

Mrs Bunthorne Look at Mr Tompkins. He's blown his moustache off.

Patty He always did have a big sneeze.

Mrs Bunthorne Wait a minute. *(She has a close look at him)* You're not really an old man, are you?

Lenny *(Bluffing desperately)* No, I'm an alien from another galaxy. I might look young, but I'm actually two hundred and fifty.

Mrs Bunthorne *(Looking closely at Patty)* And you're not old either. *(She takes off Patty's wig)* You're too young to be working here. All of you. I've no choice but to close 'Crumbs' down.

Maria Oh, please don't.

Clare We love working here.

Mrs Bunthorne I'm afraid it's against the law.

Patty What will Mrs Foster do now?

Mrs Bunthorne I'm sorry, but the shop must be closed.

Mr Bunthorne *enters with* **Mum**.

Mr Bunthorne I thought I recognized your voice, dear.

Mrs Bunthorne What are you doing here?

Mr Bunthorne Looking for someone to do the wedding. And I think I've found them. Isn't the food here smashing?

Maria Exactly.

Mrs Bunthorne It's no good, Horatio, I've got to close them down.

ACT ONE

Mr Bunthorne But they make the best cakes in town.

Clare You've got to let us stay open.

Mrs Bunthorne Impossible. You're too young to handle dangerous machinery.

Mum There isn't any machinery here. My husband's got all of that.

Maria We make everything by hand.

Clare That's why it tastes so good.

Mrs Bunthorne *(To Mum)* You're taking advantage of these young people's good nature. You're exploiting them.

Clare We're not being exploited. We want to be here.

Patty After all, wouldn't everyone jump at the chance of working with me?

Lenny And we wouldn't be too young on Alpha Centauri. You can start work when you're five there.

Everyone looks at Lenny. He shuts up.

Mum Now the business has got going, they're all receiving good pay. There's nothing else for them to do during the school holidays round here.

Mr Bunthorne And they do make exceedingly good cakes.

Mrs Bunthorne I don't know. It's very irregular.

Mr Bunthorne But you do know what Mary will be like if we don't have a good caterer for the wedding.

Mrs Bunthorne Well, yes . . .

Mr Bunthorne She'll call the whole thing off.

Mrs Bunthorne That's as may be . . .

Mr Bunthorne	She'll go on living with us.
Mrs Bunthorne	There is that possibility . . .
Mr Bunthorne	And I don't think she'll be very happy when she finds it was you who closed the one good bakers down.

>***Mrs Bunthorne** stands thinking for a moment.*
>*Everyone looks hopefully at her.*

Mrs Bunthorne	Very well. On condition that you get some older employees when the school term starts again, Mrs Foster.
Mum	Of course.
Mr Bunthorne	That settles that, then. Now let's sort out the details of the wedding breakfast . . .

>***Patty** and **Mum** take notes.*

We'll want Black Forest gateaux, orange cheesecakes, cherry meringues, chocolate eclairs . . .

Mrs Bunthorne	Horatio! We've got to give the guests a first course.
Mr Bunthorne	That *is* the first course, dear. Now for afters, can we have a lemon drizzle cake, some fudge fingers . . .

>*While **Mr** and **Mrs Bunthorne** give instructions to the rest, **Maria** and **Clare** come to one side of the kitchen.*

Maria	At least 'Crumbs' survives to fight another day.
Clare	And we've outwitted that awful Rick Beck.
Maria	Hmmm . . . but I've got a feeling we haven't heard the last of him yet.

Act 2

Scene 1

The kitchen of the bakery, some days later. **Clare** *is mixing a cake,* **Patty** *is icing another one,* **Lenny** *is kneading some dough, while* **Vicky** *whizzes on and off with a box of sandwiches.*
Patty stops, yawns and sits down.

Lenny What do you think you're doing?

Patty Having a breather. We great artistes must pace ourselves.

Lenny Well, don't let Supermouth catch you, or we'll never hear the last of it.

> *Tracy skates on and starts to make up a box of sandwiches.*

Patty You know, I don't think I'm enjoying this as much as in the early days.

Clare We're getting a very good wage.

Patty Money doesn't interest a genius.

Tracy It was better when we were doing it for fun.

Lenny It was better when Maria didn't think she was Lady Muck.

Clare It's not her fault. She's worried about the end of the holidays. She wants the shop to be doing well by the time we finish. That's why this wedding reception's important.

Tracy Yeah, but there's no need for her to be so bossy all the time. Mrs Foster's still nice to us.

Lenny You know what it reminds me of?

Patty What, dear heart?

Lenny	'Alien Space Tomatoes Ate My Wife.' Brilliant film. In that, the Chief Tomato started out perfectly normal and friendly but as it began to lead the conquest of new planets, it gradually became power mad. It started to push around all the other tomatoes it'd grown up with, till they got sick of it.
Clare	What did they do?
Lenny	Secretly sold it to a ketchup company.
Tracy	Lenny.
Lenny	Yeah?
Tracy	Shut up.
Lenny	Right.
Patty	*(Looking offstage. She gets up and goes back to work)* Look out. Here comes the Chief Tomato.

Maria enters. She is now wearing a blue overall, which marks her out from the others. She is carrying a notepad and pen. For a moment she stands, watching the others busily working. Then she goes up to Clare.

Maria	Too many sultanas.
Clare	We've always used this many.
Maria	Then we're going to have to change. It's too expensive.
Clare	But the cakes won't be as nice.
Maria	Never mind that. We've got to have an adequate profit margin.
Clare	What?
Maria	*(Annoyed)* Use fewer sultanas!

She moves to Lenny.

ACT TWO

Maria You're making the loaves too big.

Lenny They're always this size.

Maria You're to start making them ten per cent smaller.

Lenny At the same price?

Maria Yes.

Lenny That's fiddling.

Maria It's nothing of the sort. Customers actually prefer a smaller, more delicate loaf. If we charged any less for it, they would think it was poor quality.

She goes up to Tracy.

Come on, that order should have gone out ages ago.

Tracy I'm going as fast as I can.

Maria Then we'll have to see if we can find someone who can go faster.

*Tracy goes off grumpily as **Vicky** re-enters.*

Ah, Vicky, I've been meaning to talk to you.

Vicky What is it?

Maria You've taken twelve minutes to deliver a sandwich to West Street. It should only have taken nine.

Vicky It's a hot day. I came back slowly.

Maria Time is money.

Vicky I don't like rushing about.

Maria But you like the money you're paid. Here's your next order. *(Tears sheet off notepad)* Now get a move on.

> *She goes up to **Patty**, while **Vicky** starts collecting her new order in a very sulky fashion.*

Maria   That's far too fancy. You only need to put a few squiggles round the edge of the cake.

Patty   *(Horrified)* A few squiggles?

Maria   Just squidge it on.

Patty   An artiste does not 'squidge'. This is a creation.

Maria   You're only icing a birthday cake.

Patty   I am producing a masterpiece. It can't be rushed.

Maria   Well, I say it can, and while my family's paying your wages, what I say goes. Hurry up and finish it.

> ***Patty** takes off her cap and overall and goes to hang them up.*

What do you think you're doing? It's not tea-break.

Patty   I'm not going for a tea-break, Maria.

Maria   Then what are you doing?

Patty   I'm leaving. I've finished.

Maria   You can't.

Patty   I can and I will. No one, not even an old friend like you, talks to me like that.

Maria   How dare you!

Patty   *(About to exit)* If you ever become the old Maria again, you know where to find me.

> *She exits. **Clare**, **Lenny** and **Vicky** look at **Maria**.*

ACT TWO 55

Maria	*(Angry)* She always was afraid of hard work . . . What are you all looking at? Everyone needs to work harder if things are going to be ready for the wedding reception. Come on, get cracking!
	Clare, Lenny and Vicky reluctantly get back to work, while Maria takes over icing the cake that Patty left.

Scene 2

The café. Rick and Elaine are seated at a table, with coffee and different cakes on it. Rick is looking very pleased.

Rick	Only another week of the school holidays to go, my little sugar-drop?
Elaine	I think so, yes.
Rick	And then, I suppose, 'Crumbs' will have to close down. It's been such a brave experiment.
Elaine	I don't think it'll be closing, actually.
Rick	*(Taking bite of cake)* No?
Elaine	No. My sister's had some good luck. She's going to do the catering for the wedding of the Lord Mayor's daughter.

Rick	*(Spluttering on cake)* What?
Elaine	It'll be the biggest do this town's seen for years. Everyone'll get to know about 'Crumbs' now. Isn't that great for Mum and Maria?
Rick	*(Through gritted teeth)* Super.
Elaine	You're not angry, are you? Because they've got the job, and not Beck's Bakeries? It'll mean Mum can keep 'Crumbs' going even when the rest go back to school.
Rick	It's simply wonderful news. You know, I think I'd like to congratulate your sister personally.
Elaine	Really?
Rick	Yes . . . *(Thinking rapidly)* You know, I'm rather afraid your sister got the impression in the past that I didn't want her business to succeed . . .
Elaine	You did try to get it closed down . . .
Rick	*(Ignoring her)* So I'd like to make up for any misunderstanding. Will you tell her to come up to the warehouse with you at six o'clock this evening?
Elaine	Why?
Rick	I've thought of a big favour I can do her. It'll save her a lot of money.
Elaine	Rick, you wouldn't try tricking her, would you?
Rick	Me? How could you think such a thing? I've only got the best interests of your family at heart, Elaine. You do believe me, don't you?
Elaine	*(Slight hesitation)* Yes, Rick.

*****Rick** smiles, then snaps like a wolf at a cake.*

Scene 3

The kitchen of the bakery. **Lenny** *and* **Clare** *are changing out of their overalls.* **Vicky** *and* **Tracy** *are standing with their skateboards under their arms, staring at Maria. There has obviously been an argument.*

Maria *(To Vicky and Tracy)* I hope I've made myself clear. If you two aren't prepared to work faster tomorrow, don't bother turning up.

Vicky and Tracy look at each other.

Vicky and Tracy We won't!

They exit angrily.

Clare Maria, don't you think . . .

Maria I don't want to hear any more whingeing today. Just make sure both of you are here half an hour early tomorrow so that we can get everything baked for the wedding reception.

Clare and Lenny shrug their shoulders at each other.

Clare Goodnight, Maria.

Lenny Goodnight.

Mrs Foster enters. Clare and Lenny say goodbye to her as they exit.

Mum Goodnight Clare, goodnight Lenny.

Mum comes down to Maria.

So Tracy and Vicky are leaving now?

Maria Good riddance.

Mum And Patty.

Maria We're better off without them.

Mum	They've been good friends to you.
Maria	They're workshy, that's the trouble.
Mum	Are you sure the fault's in them? *(She puts her arm round Maria)* Don't you think you've been a bit too hard on everyone lately?
Maria	I know, Mum . . . but how else could we get the business to succeed?
Mum	It doesn't cost anything to be nice to people.
Maria	If you're nice, people think you're soft. Look at Rick Beck. In the early days, he thought he could bully us into closing down. Now he knows we're made of tougher stuff, he's going out of his way to do us favours.
Mum	What do you mean?
Maria	I'm going to meet him and Elaine at his warehouse. Apparently he knows a way we can save money.
Mum	Now, you don't trust him for one minute, do you?
Maria	I'm more than a match for him, don't worry. But he's afraid of the competition we're giving him, that's why he wants to get into our good books.
Mum	He's a very crafty character.
Maria	I'll get the better of him.
Mum	I hope so.
Maria	Mum . . . you know I'm doing this . . . for all of us. To prove that you, me and Elaine can stand on our own feet without Dad.
Mum	I know, dear, but sometimes I wish . . .
Maria	What?
Mum	You were a bit more like your old self.

Maria	*(Looks at watch)* I'd better get going. *(She hangs up her overall)* Don't worry, Mum . . . We'll be all right.

She exits. Mum shakes her head sadly.

Scene 4

Rick's warehouse. **Rick** is standing with a big, open bag of flour. He takes out a handful, sniffs it and pulls a face at the smell. He quickly puts the flour back in the sack as he hears **Elaine** and **Maria** entering.

Rick	Hello Sweetie-pie . . . *(Extending hand to Maria)* Congratulations, Miss Foster.
Maria	*(Reluctantly shakes his hand, then wipes off the flour on her skirt)* Congratulations on what?
Rick	Congratulations on making such a success of 'Crumbs'. I hear some of your products are almost as good as my own.

Maria	They're a lot better.
Elaine	Don't be rude, Maria. He only wants to help.
Rick	And special congratulations on being chosen to do the Bunthorne wedding.
Maria	How did you know? Elaine . . .
Rick	It's the talk of the whole town, Miss Foster. 'Crumbs' is becoming famous.
Maria	No thanks to you.
Rick	I've realized Beck's Bakeries is going to have to put up with you being around for a long time . . .
Maria	We will be.
Rick	So I've decided to come to an arrangement with you.
Maria	What do you mean?
Rick	I won't try and buy your shop any more.
Maria	Or snitch to the Health Inspectors?
Elaine	Maria!
Rick	In fact, as a gesture of goodwill, I'm willing to do a very good deal on some flour with you.
Maria	Why?
Rick	Just as a favour. After all, you can never be a threat to such a big company as mine.
Maria	I don't believe it's a favour.
Elaine	You're being horrible, Maria . . .

Rick	*(To Elaine)* No, your sister's being smart. She knows there's always a reason for doing things in the business world. *(To Maria)* To be honest with you, 'Crumbs' has been doing so well, we haven't been selling as much as usual. We've got some extra sacks of flour we want to get rid of before they go stale.
Maria	What's in it for you?
Rick	You pay us half-price. It's better than having to throw them away.
Elaine	Rick's only got your best interests at heart.
Maria	Half-price?
Rick	That's right. Think of the money you could save baking for the wedding reception.
Maria	But the Bunthornes have already paid me the full price.
Rick	So? You'd be making a little extra profit, that's all.
Elaine	Rick's ever so kindly.
Rick	I'm too soft-hearted to be a real businessman.
Maria	It really would be half-price?
Rick	Scout's honour.
Maria	Then it's a deal. Make sure they're delivered first thing tomorrow.
Rick	It's a pleasure to do business with you.

They shake hands.

Elaine	Thank heavens you've come to your senses at last, Maria.
Maria	*(Exiting)* First thing tomorrow, mind.
Elaine	You never told me you were a scout, Rick.
Rick	*(To himself, smiling)* I wasn't. *(He gives Elaine a big, cheesy grin)*

Scene 5

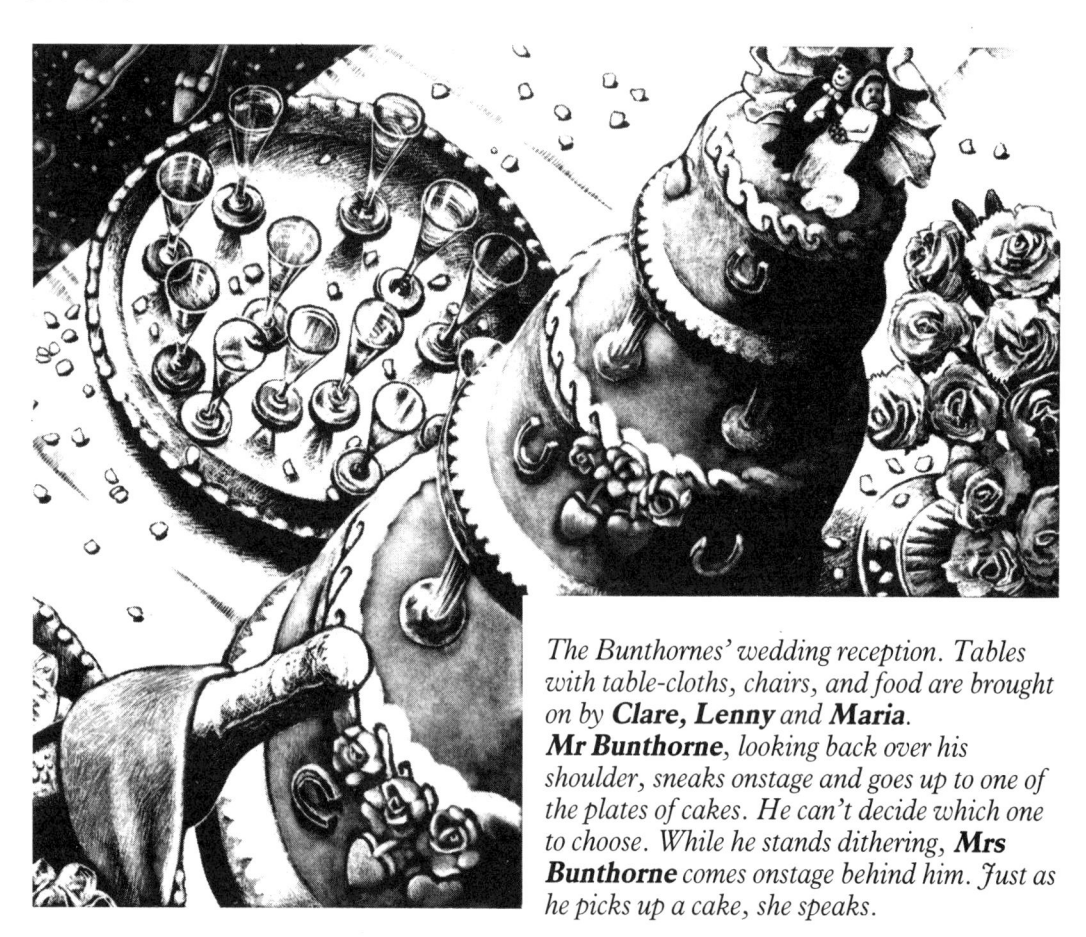

*The Bunthornes' wedding reception. Tables with table-cloths, chairs, and food are brought on by **Clare, Lenny** and **Maria**.*
***Mr Bunthorne**, looking back over his shoulder, sneaks onstage and goes up to one of the plates of cakes. He can't decide which one to choose. While he stands dithering, **Mrs Bunthorne** comes onstage behind him. Just as he picks up a cake, she speaks.*

Mrs Bunthorne There you are, Horatio!

He drops the cake.

What do you think you're doing? Everyone's waiting for the photographs outside.

Mr Bunthorne But dear, I haven't eaten for almost an hour.

Mrs Bunthorne Outside, Horatio. Mary thinks one of her tempers is coming on.

ACT TWO

Mr Bunthorne Oh no.

He hurries off with his wife.

Maria Make sure every place has one of our business cards by it.

Lenny You don't think we're overdoing it?

Maria I want everyone to know 'Crumbs' has done the catering for this wedding. We could get a lot of business out of the publicity.

Clare It's a shame we didn't make things properly, then.

Maria What do you mean?

Clare That cheap flour was horrible.

Maria It was perfectly all right. The cakes look lovely.

Lenny How come none of us has had the courage to try them?

Clare *(Looking off)* I think they're ready to come in.

Maria Places, everyone.

Lenny Aye, aye, Skipper.

*They stand out of the way as **Mary** and **Archibald**, followed by **Mr** and **Mrs Bunthorne**, lead the wedding guests in. **Mary** is clearly in charge.*

Mary Go and sit there, Archibald . . . Mother, Father, you go and sit there . . . *(To the rest of the guests)* Now you sit there . . . you go over there . . . Do hurry, please. *(She goes to join Archibald)* Take your elbows off the table, Archibald, and sit up straight. Honestly.

***Mr Bunthorne** has sat down and is about to start eating a plate of cakes. **Mrs Bunthorne**, standing next to him, slaps his hand.*

Mrs Bunthorne	Wait, Horatio! *(To the guests)* Ladies and gentlemen, before we start the meal, my husband would like to say a few words. Come on Horatio.
Mr Bunthorne	*(Getting up)* Oh, very well . . . *(Addressing guests)* Now, there's no reason why you can't be tucking in, even though I can't . . .

> *Everyone starts eating, except for **Archibald**, who simply looks miserable, **Mrs Bunthorne**, who's too intent on what her husband's saying, and **Clare**, **Lenny** and **Maria**.*

First of all, I'd just like to say, thanks for coming. I'd like to say a big thank you to 'Crumbs' bakery for doing all this food, that I can hardly wait to try . . .

> ***Mrs Bunthorne** coughs reprovingly.*

. . . Er . . . it's a very special day for me and the wife. We feel we're not losing a daughter, we're gaining a sultana cake . . . sorry, a son-in-law . . . and I'd like to wish the happy couple a long and happy lunch together . . . er, I mean, life together . . . Excuse me, I simply must try a fondant fancy . . .

> *He picks up and bites a cake.*

. . . Absolutely delicious . . . and in closing, I'd like to say . . .

> *He's finding it harder and harder to talk, as the cake is turning to cement in his mouth. The same thing is happening to everyone else eating.*

. . . ot a reaggy wongerfoog . . . og . . . og . . . og . . .

> *His mouth has become absolutely set.*

Mrs Bunthorne	Horatio, what's wrong?

> *She looks at his mouth and the half-eaten cake in his hand.*

ACT TWO

Mrs Bunthorne Quick drying cement! Don't anyone touch the food. This is the fault of 'Crumbs' bakery!

> *Mary stands up. She is obviously furious, but cannot speak. As Archibald realizes this, he begins to look a bit happier.*

Clare What's happening, Maria? What's gone wrong?

> *Rick enters. He goes to Mrs Bunthorne.*

Rick Excuse me. I'm from Beck's Bakeries. I hear you've got a problem with the food . . .

Maria You dirty double-crosser!

Rick . . . And I happened to be passing with a vanful of delicious Beck's sandwiches and cakes. Would you like me to take over the catering?

Clare You rotten cheat!

Mrs Bunthorne *(To Rick)* Thank you very much. The first thing you can do is throw that dreadful 'Crumbs' food away.

Maria *(Goes up to Mrs Bunthorne)* But you don't understand . . .

Mrs Bunthorne Go away, you horrible little girl!

Mr Bunthorne Gog away yo oggigle giggle girg!

Maria But . . .

Mrs Bunthorne Go away!

> *Maria, Lenny and Clare start to walk off in despair. Everyone is staring nastily, or shaking their fists at them, except for Archibald, who pats them gratefully on the head as they pass by. Only he and Rick look happy.*

Scene 6

The kitchen of the bakery. **Mum** *is putting the mixing bowls into a cardboard box.* **Lenny** *and* **Clare** *carry on the 'Crumbs' sign, dump it on the floor, and help start packing things up.* **Maria** *is sitting very sadly on a chair.*

Mum   Don't feel so upset about it, Maria.

Maria   It's all my fault.

Mum   No, it's not.

Clare   It's that sneaky rat Rick's fault.

Lenny   If only we could prove it.

Tracy and Vicky enter.

Tracy   Hiya.

Vicky   We heard you're closing.

Tracy   We're sorry.

Mum   Poor old Maria was tricked into a bad deal.

Lenny   Now we've got the worst reputation in the whole of the cosmos.

Clare   Lenny!

Maria   I should've had more sense . . . I was getting greedy . . . I was awful to everyone . . .

Lenny   Just like the Chief Tomato.

Maria   *(To Tracy and Vicky)* Especially to you two and poor old Patty, and look where it's got me in the end. I've ruined the business.

Mum   Selling it's probably the best thing that could have happened. With the money Beck's are paying for it, I'm going to start up a new business.

ACT TWO

Clare What sort of business?

Mum I don't know yet. But one thing this summer's proved to me is there's no reason why I shouldn't make a success of one.

Maria As long as you learn from my mistakes and don't get power-mad.

Tracy Will you need help at the weekends?

Mum I might do.

Vicky Count us in.

Clare And me.

Lenny And me.

Mum The best thing is that Elaine's coming in with me.

Clare What about her and Rick?

Mum After the way he behaved at the wedding, I think she's seeing him in a new light. She insisted on handling the sale of this place herself.

. . . .

Scene 7

*The café. **Rick** and **Elaine** are seated at a table. There is a pot of coffee, cups and a large creamy cake on the middle of the table. **Rick** hands some official-looking papers to Elaine.*

Rick There you are, Lambkins. Sign at the bottom and I'll give you a lovely cheque for your little shop.

Elaine *(Very business-like)* You've made a mistake. This should be five thousand pounds more.

She points the mistake out to him and he corrects it.

Rick	Oh yes . . . how silly of me . . . I'm glad you noticed.
	Elaine signs it; keeps one copy of the document herself and gives the other back to him. She takes the cheque from him.
Elaine	*(Getting up)* I think that's everything.
Rick	Aren't you staying for coffee?
Elaine	No, I'm not.
Rick	Not even for a slice of delicious Beck's cream cake?
Elaine	You know, that cake does look very tempting.
Rick	Of course it does.
Elaine	I think I will try it.
Rick	*(Offering her the plate)* Go ahead.
	Elaine pushes the cake straight into his face.
Elaine	You know, that's the first time I can honestly say I've enjoyed one of your cakes. *(She starts to exit)* Goodbye Rick. For ever. *(Exits)*

· ·

Scene 8

The kitchen of the bakery. Everything is packed up ready to leave. **Lenny, Clare, Mum, Maria, Tracy** *and* **Vicky** *are about to go.*
Patty sweeps onstage.

Patty	What's this wonderful news I hear, darlings?
Maria	There is no wonderful news. 'Crumbs' is closing down.
Patty	What does that matter, when you're back to your normal self? That's the absolutely fan-tastic news.

Lenny	And I can see *you're* back to your normal self.
Mum	Well, let's say goodbye to the old place. It's the last time we'll see it.
Clare	I'll miss working here. It's been the best summer of my life.
Vicky	I can't wait for you to start up something new, Mrs Foster.

Elaine enters.

Elaine	I've got the cheque, Mum.
Maria	Let's cash it before it bounces.
Patty	You're going to start a new business?
Mum	Yes, though we don't know what, yet.
Patty	Let me see . . . This is where we creative geniuses are so important . . . What sort of business could it be . . . ?

She goes into a world of her own as the others start to leave.

It's coming to me, it's coming to me . . . I can see it now . . . 'Patty's Pizza Parlour', with marble tables, tanks of fish set into the walls . . . a multi-coloured fountain in the middle of the restaurant . . . No, no, it should be something more ambitious . . . 'Patty's Fashion House', the envy of Paris, of the world . . . What do you think? *(She turns and sees that everyone has gone)* Wait for me! You can't do anything without a genius!

She exits. Finish.

Activities

Women and Work	72
'You Are What You Read'	76
Divorce	77
Chainstores	79
Takeover	81
All Power Corrupts	82
News Story	83
Child Labour	84
Day-dreams and Ambition	86
Drama Ideas	88
Performing 'Hot Cakes'	90
What the Playwright Says	91
Acknowledgements	93

Women and Work

Rick Beck

Let's face it: women shouldn't have to worry their pretty little heads about business, should they?

The belief that some jobs aren't suited to women is still surprisingly common. For example, the vast majority of the Members of Parliament in Britain are men, although over fifty per cent of the population is female. It's also still rare to have women judges, high-ranking police officers or company directors.

Attitudes have varied at different times in our history, too. During the First and Second World Wars, women in Britain took on all sorts of work, in factories and on farms. Previously, it had been considered too demanding for them to do, but in wartime, a woman's ability to work hard was too important to ignore.

ACTIVITIES

Nowadays, thirty-six per cent of Britain's workforce are women. The economy would collapse without them, yet women are still, on average, paid less than men. What's more, women who work at home, as housewives and mothers, have no fixed wage at all, but may work longer hours than anyone else!

Write

Look at these types of worker: nurse, teacher, garage mechanic, surgeon, cleaner, chef, secretary, train driver, school cook.

Draw up a table with three headings – 'usually female', 'usually male', 'either' – and divide the list up. Add any other types of job you can think of yourself.

Talk

1 'Men's jackets button on the right, women's jackets on the left.'
'Gentlemen should walk on the outside.'
'You should stand up when a lady enters a room.'

What other 'rules' of behaviour do we have that depend on our gender? Is there any point to them?

2 In a debate, two teams of speakers argue for and against a particular proposition.
Choose two speakers for and two speakers against the following proposition:

'Men and women should be equal in all things.'

Each speaker is allowed two minutes to make their case. The rest of the group can make any points they want to after the four main speakers.
End by taking a vote on the proposition.

Improvise

In pairs, improvise the following scenes:

1. Between a mother and a daughter: the mother is worried that her daughter isn't sufficiently 'ladylike' and decides to raise the matter one evening.

2. Between an employer and a female employee: the employee approaches her boss for a pay rise – she feels she would be earning more if she were a man doing the same job. The boss doesn't want to grant the rise. Show what happens.

Read

Ballad of a Dreamy Girl

A pigtail dangled down my back,
I was just sixteen years.
One day my mother came and flicked
a duster round my ears.

'Don't sit there writing poetry,
go dust your room instead!
With all this nonsense you won't earn
the butter on your bread!'

She often scolded me, but I
stepped lightly as a bird
and went on dreaming through the day
as if I had not heard.

What could I say? My mother
would never understand.
So I wrote only secretly,
the duster in my hand.

When finally I learned to cook,
I often heard her tell:
'To keep your future husband sweet,
you'll have to feed him well!'

'And how do men keep women sweet?'
She gave me no reply
but went on cooking, and I saw
her shake her head and sigh.

Edith Roseveare

Talk

1. Who does the housework in your home? Why?

2. Why did the writer's mother think her daughter should be doing housework? Would she have thought the same if she'd had a son?

3. Why do you think the mother sighs and shakes her head at the end of the poem?

ACTIVITIES 75

4 Do you think that women are generally expected to keep men 'sweet'? If so, in what ways?

Write Make a list of all the skills you think teenage boys and teenage girls should learn to prepare them for later life. Are they the same skills for boys and girls?

'You Are What You Read'

There are more teenage magazines aimed at girls than at boys. Many of them have a similar style and content – concentrating on fashion, love and pop music.

Talk   Conduct a survey to find out what magazines and comics your classmates like to read. Ask them to say what they most like or dislike about them. What is the favourite? Which is the least well-liked?

Write   Choose one or two magazines to review. How do girls appear in them? What are the boys in them like? Say whether you find the magazine interesting and enjoyable or not, and give your reasons.

Design   Draw or design the front cover of a new teenage magazine that reflects your own interests. List the contents it would have.
In a group, you could make up one issue of the new magazine with drawings, articles and even a photo-story, if your school has photographic facilities.

ACTIVITIES

Divorce

Maria It was great . . . in the old days. When Dad came in for tea. He was always smiling, especially at Mum. She'd smile back at him when she thought me and 'Laine weren't looking – a secret little smile.

Clare What happened?

Maria Somehow they just stopped smiling . . . And one day Dad told us he was leaving.

- Approximately one marriage in three in Britain now ends in divorce.
- The divorce rate in Britain is almost twice as high as the European average.
- Most, though not all, children affected by a divorce say they wish their parents had stayed together, even if it meant more arguments at home.
- Usually the mother gets custody of the children after a divorce.
- Within a couple of years of divorce, a high number of fathers have stopped seeing their children altogether.
- Most children affected by a divorce feel they didn't really have the reasons for it happening explained to them.

Talk

1 What do you think are the main reasons for people getting divorced?

2 Why do you think some parents lose touch with their children after a divorce?

3 What causes the most arguments between girlfriends and boyfriends?

4 What are your own views on marriage? Is it still an important institution? Do you think you'll marry one day?

Write

Imagine that Maria writes to her grandparents at the time of her parents' divorce. What would she say in the letter to describe her own feelings, those of her sister and her parents' feelings as well?

Improvise

1 **In pairs:** a boyfriend and girlfriend meet up. One of them has decided to tell the other it's time for the relationship to finish. What happens?

2 **In groups:** create a family scene, in which the parents tell their children for the first time that they're thinking of separating or getting a divorce. How do they break the news? Do the children think it's a good idea or not?

Chainstores

In the play, Beck's Bakeries set out to buy up 'Crumbs' and turn it into another one of its chain of shops.

Chainstores – that is, shops owned by the same company, selling the same sort of goods – go back at least until 1643, when a group of pharmacy shops was set up in Japan.

However, it is really in the second half of the Twentieth Century, with the advent of mass production and automation in factories, that chain stores have become most successful. F. W. Woolworth's and Marks and Spencer's are two of the best known chains, with shops in most major towns in the country.

With the rise of the large national and even international shops, there has been a change in our shopping habits. People tend to go less often to the small, specialist shops. Many small local shops have been forced to close in recent years, particularly in city centres.

Talk

In pairs, answer these questions:

1. What chainstores would you expect to find in most city centres?
2. Can you remember any shops that have closed down near where you live? If so, why do you think they closed?
3. What are the good points about chainstores? What are the good points about small, locally-owned shops?
4. Which shops do you usually go to? What do you like most about them?
5. How do shops try to affect the customers' moods when they're shopping?

Write

A big new superstore is being built near where you live. Some local residents are against it, because they think it will force other shops out of business and will bring a lot of traffic into the area. Other residents are all in favour of it, saying it will increase choice when shopping.

Decide what your opinion is and send a letter to your local newspaper saying what you think should happen.

Design

In the play, Patty produces a shop sign for 'Crumbs', which Rick Beck calls 'amateurish'.

Think of a name for a shop you would like to run yourself, and design a sign for it. Create a logo to go on the shop's carrier bags and publicity. Draw up an advertisement for the shop to go into a newspaper.

Act

Make up an advertisement for 'Crumbs' or for your own shop, which you can then record on cassette or videotape.

ACTIVITIES   81

Takeover

Mrs Bunthorne   What are you doing here?

Mr Bunthorne   Looking for someone to do the wedding. And I think I've found them. Isn't the food here smashing?

Rick Beck denies that he regards 'Crumbs' as direct competition for his own business, but it's clear that he does. 'Crumbs' bread and cakes are popular because they taste good. Even if Rick Beck reduces the price of his bread and cakes people may still prefer to buy at 'Crumbs'. The only way that he can keep his customers is to take over the business.

Improvise It's a Saturday morning, and you have gone out to buy food. When you arrive at 'Crumbs' you discover that it's closed. There is a sign in the window announcing that the shop has been taken over by Beck's Bakeries. You know that Beck's bread is cheaper but you don't like the taste. 'Crumbs' was the only good bakery in the area. Other shoppers are discussing the takeover. How do you feel? What do you decide to do?

Discuss If you had been in Rick Beck's position, what would *you* have done? Remember that your first aim must be to keep your own company in business.

All Power Corrupts

There is a famous saying: 'All power corrupts, and absolute power corrupts absolutely' – meaning that anyone who has any sort of power will be changed by it, and changed for the worse.

During **Hot Cakes** this happens to Maria. At the beginning of the play she takes on the running of the bakery, just to prove to her mother that they can succeed without her father to help them. However, slowly she begins to change . . .

Write

Write two entries for Maria's diary: one from Act 1, and one from Act 2. See if you can bring out the changes in Maria's personality not just by *what* you write, but also by the *way* you write it.

Maria's character isn't the only one that changes in the course of the play. You might also like to write diary entries for Mrs Foster, or for Elaine. Look back at the play for evidence about their characters at the beginning of **Hot Cakes**, and at the end.

Debate

In your class or group, discuss the idea that 'All power corrupts'. (You can turn this into a formal debate if you like; your teacher will help you to organize this.) Before you begin, you might like to select a few people to act as 'journalists' who will write a report on the discussion afterwards, or you might like to use a tape-recorder to record it.

Alternatively, you could use both journalists *and* a tape recorder. When the journalists have presented their report, play the tape again, and see how the written version differs from the one on tape.

At the end of the discussion, take a vote.

ACTIVITIES

News Story

Write

You are a journalist working on a local paper. You have just heard that Rick Beck has taken over 'Crumbs' following the Bunthornes' disastrous wedding reception, and your editor wants you to cover the story. But you have your own ideas about how you're going to do it.

Choose one of the following options, then write your news story:

1. You're a friend of the Bunthornes, and you are horrified that the wedding reception was ruined.

2. You secretly admire Rick Beck – he may be ruthless but he is very successful, and you've been hoping for the opportunity to write a profile of this top young businessman for months. Now you've got your chance to interview him.

3. Your sister is at school with Maria Foster, so you know all about her attempts to keep 'Crumbs' going, and make a success of the business. Even though she has failed, you decide to write her story.

4. You've heard of a group of local people who have got together to protest about the closure of 'Crumbs'. They are backed by the Campaign for Real Bread, and they are planning a series of demonstrations outside Beck's Bakeries' shops. You go to see them in action.

5. You're writing a series of articles about local women in business. You've heard that Mrs Foster, once the proprietor of 'Crumbs' bakery, is starting up another business. What is it?

6. You're the local crime reporter, but apart from a few burglaries nothing much seems to happen in your area. However, a friend of yours, who works as a security guard at Beck's warehouse, saw Rick Beck preparing to sell Maria Foster a consignment of sub-standard flour as a 'favour'. You have long suspected that Rick Beck may be a shady character. This could be your first big story . . .

Child Labour

Mrs Bunthorne Wait a minute. You're not really an old man, are you? . . . And you're not old either. You're too young to be working here. All of you. I've no choice but to close 'Crumbs' down.

In 1933 the Children and Young Person's Act stated that no young person in the United Kingdom could be employed:

a so long as he is under the age of thirteen;
b before the end of school hours or for more than two hours on any day he is required to be at school;
c before 7 a.m. or 7 p.m. on any day; or
d for more than two hours on a Sunday; or
e be required to lift, carry or move anything so heavy as to be likely to cause injury to him.

There has not always been legal protection to stop children from working long hours, or doing dangerous jobs. During the Industrial Revolution, many children worked in the newly created factories, often with dangerous machinery, for very low wages. Unscrupulous employers used them as a cheap and easily controlled source of labour. Young children were even sent to work in the mines, until 1842 when a law was passed that stopped anyone under ten years old from working underground.

As a result of increasing legal protection, few children in Britain today are made to work against their will. Part-time work – serving in a shop or delivering papers, for example – can be a useful source of spending money and can help foster independence.

ACTIVITIES

In contrast, in many of the economically poorer countries of the world, children still work full-time. It is estimated that in some countries of the Middle East, they make up ten per cent of the workforce. Parts of Latin America and Asia also depend to a considerable degree on child labour. The families of those children may depend on the wages they earn for food and other essentials.

Write

Conduct a survey amongst the pupils in your school, of the different part-time jobs they do. Which are the best paid? Which are the most interesting? How did they find their jobs?

Research

Find out from your parents and grandparents what types of work they did when they were young.

Improvise

One of the delivery girls at 'Crumbs' is involved in an accident when delivering sandwiches. The police want to know why Mrs Foster has been employing such a young work force. Act out the interview which will decide whether or not she is going to be prosecuted.

Day-dreams and Ambition

Patty

I can see it now . . . 'Patty's Pizza Parlour', with marble tables, tanks of fish set into the walls . . . a multi-coloured fountain in the middle of the restaurant . . . No, no, it should be something more ambitious . . . 'Patty's Fashion House', the envy of Paris, the world . . . What do you think? (*She turns and sees that everyone has gone*) Wait for me! You can't do anything without a genius!

Everyone day-dreams part of the time. We imagine exciting events that might happen in our lives – becoming a famous pop-star, winning an Olympic medal, or being in charge of the school for a day.

Some people set about making their day-dreams come true. Perhaps they work hard at learning to play an instrument and form a pop-group with their friends. Perhaps they train at an athletics club and develop their natural ability to the point where they win races. In this way, a day-dream becomes a real ambition that may actually be achieved.

ACTIVITIES

Write

Make a list of at least three ambitions you have in life. Under each one, write down the steps you will have to take to achieve that ambition. For example:

> I want to become an actor.
>
> I need to:
> Take part in school productions.
> Perhaps join a local amateur drama group.
> Find out from a teacher or careers officer how to train to become professional.
> Read about actors' lives or, better still, meet and talk to some, to see if it's what I really want.

There are plenty of other ambitions – to travel the world; to become an engineer, a doctor, a footballer; to learn how to sail. What are yours?

Talk

What do you think are the main differences between a day-dream and an ambition?

If you could have anything in the world happen to make your day-dream come true, what would it be?

Do you think it is dangerous to day-dream too much?

Design

Patty day-dreams of becoming a fashion designer. Remembering her flamboyant character, sketch two men's outfits and two women's outfits she might design.

Suggest which materials they would be made out of and show the colours she'd use.

Improvise

1. Lenny is constantly day-dreaming about space monsters. Act out a scene in which he comes into the bakery one morning and finds there's a space monster already there.

2. After a careers talk, a boy or girl comes home and announces what he or she would like to be after leaving school. The family doesn't take this seriously. How does the boy/girl try to convince them that it's a real ambition and not just a day-dream?

Drama Ideas

1 Ageing yourself

There are a number of ways to make yourself appear older more successfully than Maria and her friends managed.
Appropriate costume and stage make-up, if put on carefully, can help.

It is helpful to think of the ways in which older people move, sit, and talk. Try to think of some real older people you know.

On your own: imagine an older person whom you are going to become. Find a way for that character to speak and move. Perhaps you can find a suitable costume.
Imagine what that character has done during her or his life. What memories are most important to them?

In groups: have a 'This is Your Life' session. In character as an older person, you must answer questions about your life and times. If asked, you must be prepared to act out scenes from your past life, using other members of the group as friends and relatives.
This takes a lot of quick thinking, but is great fun.

2 Work

In a group: Maria and her friends work in sequence to make sandwiches. Think of a job like this that needs teamwork – like building a car, or decorating a room. Choose one movement each which you can easily repeat and start moving in sequence. See what effect doing it to music with a strong rhythm has.

In a group, think of a business that you would all like to set up. Create your new workplace and act out a morning's work in it – perhaps there's an awkward customer, or an accident to deal with.

3 'Nobody talks to me like that'

Patty falls out with Maria because she doesn't like being treated rudely by a friend.

In pairs, develop a situation in which two good friends have a serious disagreement. Show what happens to their friendship afterwards.

4 Families

What elements make a drama about family life interesting and enjoyable? Can you think of some examples of this type of drama on television?

In groups, create a family group – parent(s), children and other relatives. Develop a play with at least three scenes to show how this family deals with a crisis or some new challenge – perhaps a divorce or money problems.

Videotape your play, then watch it. See whether the characters you've created are believable and/or entertaining. How could you have improved the play?

Performing 'Hot Cakes'

Nothing kills an audience's interest in a play more than long, unnecessary scene changes, particularly since TV, video and cinema have made us used to a drama cutting quickly from one event to the next.

Hot Cakes has no need for such scene changes, or a complicated set. Most of the action takes place in the bakery kitchen and this could be set up onstage all the time.

The opening scene in the street could occur at the front of the stage, while Rick's warehouse can simply be suggested by the bag of flour he uses. The café and the Bunthornes' house only need a table and chairs to be brought on and off – if it's done by the actors themselves, it will speed up the action. For the wedding reception, a few table-cloths and extra chairs could transform the kitchen, temporarily, into a hall.

Only simple lighting and costume are needed to stage the play and there are no special effects. This, of course, puts an extra responsibility on the performers to keep their audience entertained by the quality of their acting!

Design

A good set should help give the audience a sense of where the play is taking place and help create an atmosphere, without distracting from the actors. Bearing this in mind, draw a plan for the bakery kitchen. What must it contain for the play to be acted out successfully?
If possible, take your design a stage further by making a small cardboard model of the set. Try and make it to scale.

Draw sketches of your ideas for the costumes the main characters could wear. Would they be dressed differently at the wedding reception to the rest of the play?

Sketch out make-up and hair-style designs for the main characters.

Act

Choose one or two scenes from the play. Find appropriate props and costume for them.
Decide what the main points of each scene are and then improvise it (without using your books) to get used to having the props. Next, try and act it out with the scripts.

What the Playwright Says

My main aim in writing **Hot Cakes** was to create a play which would be enjoyable to act out in the classroom or on the school stage. If it has you yawning and snoring by the time you're halfway through, it's definitely failed.

The idea for the play came from the increasingly common links between schools and businesses. I wondered what it would be like if a group of teenage friends did try to run their own business, not just for fun, but as a real way of establishing their independence.

All sorts of questions immediately came to mind. Can friendships survive when you become workmates? What happens if one person has to take on the role of the boss? Do you have to be thick-skinned to succeed?

In the end, **Hot Cakes** doesn't really have the answers to these, or any other questions. That's partly because I never know the answer to anything more complicated than, 'Who won the F.A. Cup in 1984?' or 'How many beans make five?' More importantly, I don't think playwrights should tell people what to think, since the average reader has twice the sense of the average playwright.

With that, I've said everything I've got to say, except that I hope you enjoy reading it and the best of luck if you perform it.

Adrian Flynn

(P.S. The answers are:
1   Everton
2   A bean and a half, a bean and a half, half a bean, and a bean and a half.)

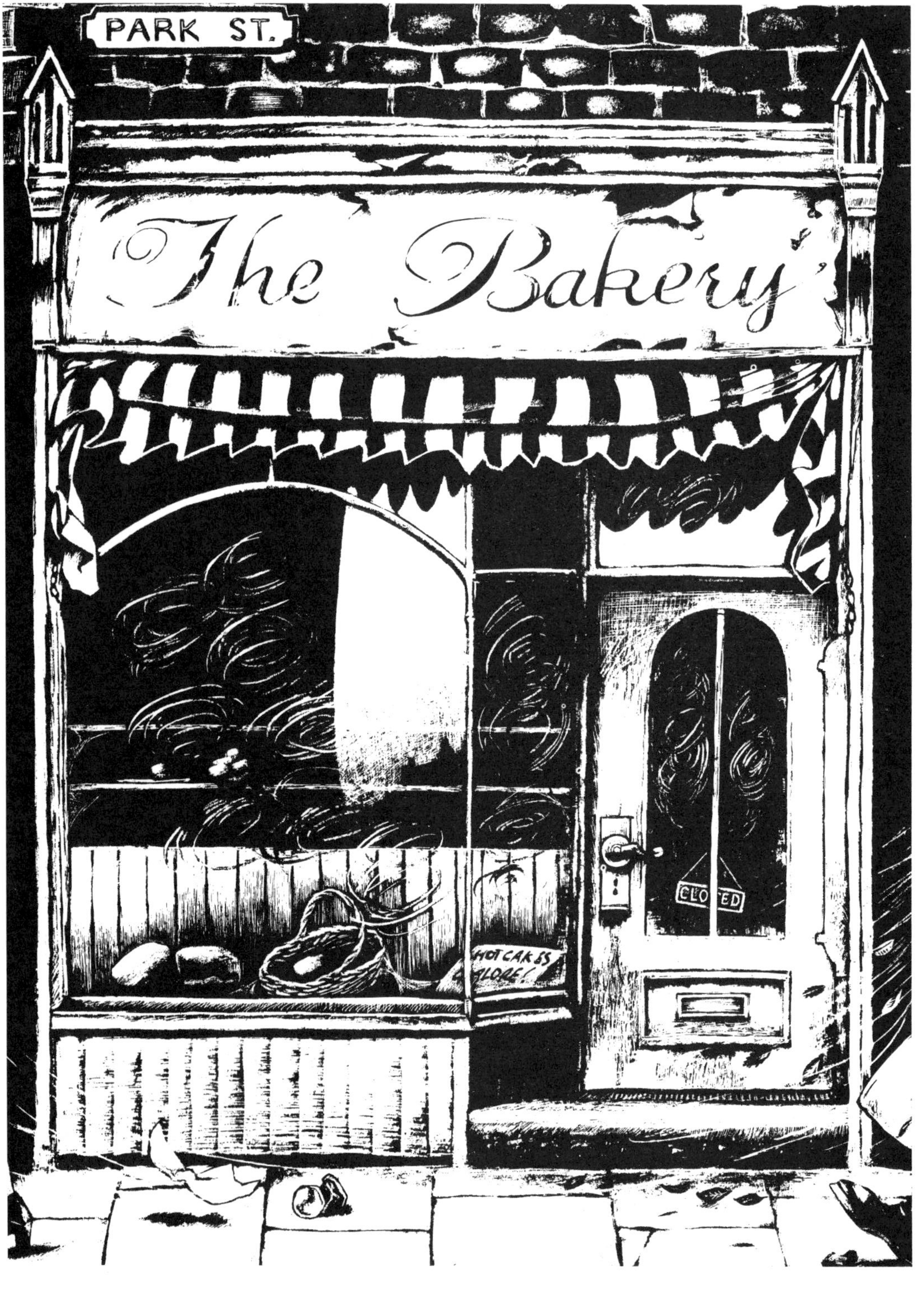
PARK ST.
The Bakery
CLOSED
HOT CAKES

ACKNOWLEDGEMENTS

'Ballad of a Dreamy Girl' by Edith Roseveare. Reprinted from *Messages*, ed. Naomi Lewis, Faber & Faber 1985, by kind permission of H. G. Roseveare.

The illustrations are by Neil Chapman and Alan Marks. The handwriting is by Elitta Fell.

The publishers would like to thank the following for permission to reproduce photographs:

Mary Evans Picture Library p72, p84; Format Partners – Photo Library p73, p80, p85; Sally and Richard Greenhill p86; Holborn Publishing Group p76 (left); Marks and Spencer plc p79; D. C. Thomson and Co. Ltd. p76 (middle).

Other plays in this series include:

Across the Barricades   ISBN 0 19 831272 5
    Joan Lingard   adapted by David Ian Neville

*The Burston School Strike   ISBN 0 19 831274 1
    Roy Nevitt

The Demon Headmaster   ISBN 0 19 831270 9
    Gillian Cross   adapted by Adrian Flynn

Frankenstein   ISBN 0 19 831267 9
    Mary Shelley   adapted by Philip Pullman

Hot Cakes   ISBN 0 19 831273 3
    Adrian Flynn

Paper Tigers   ISBN 0 19 831268 7
    Steve Barlow and Steve Skidmore

A Question of Courage   ISBN 0 19 831271 7
    Marjorie Darke   adapted by Bill Lucas and Brian Keaney

*The Teen Commandments   ISBN 0 19 831275 X
    Kelvin Reynolds

*Tigers on the Prowl   ISBN 0 19 831277 6
    Steve Barlow and Steve Skidmore

The Turbulent Term of Tyke Tiler   ISBN 0 19 831269 5
    adapted from her own novel by Gene Kemp

OXFORD *Playscripts*

Series editor:
Bill Lucas

Oxford Playscripts is a powerful series of new plays specially selected for young secondary school students.

The series features:

- *New writing from Youth Theatres, adaptations, and a range of new scripts from stage and TV.*
- *Insights into the plays by the authors.*
- *Activities on improvisation, role play, discussion, and extended writing.*
- *Relevant illustrations to act as further stimulus.*

Hot Cakes

When her parents divorce, Maria and her mother are left running a bakery. Mum wants to sell it. Maria has other ideas – but success has its price...

Other titles in the series:

Across the Barricades	ISBN 0 19 831272 5
The Bonny Pit Laddie	ISBN 0 19 831278 4
The Burston School Strike	ISBN 0 19 831274 1
The Demon Headmaster	ISBN 0 19 831270 9
Frankenstein	ISBN 0 19 831267 9
Paper Tigers	ISBN 0 19 831268 7
A Question of Courage	ISBN 0 19 831271 7
The Teen Commandments	ISBN 0 19 831275 X
Tigers on the Prowl	ISBN 0 19 831277 6
The Turbulent Term of Tyke Tiler	ISBN 0 19 831269 5

Orders and enquiries to Customer Services:

tel. 01536 741519
fax. 01536 454519

Oxford University Press

ISBN 0-19-831273-3

9 780198 312734